Silent
Power

BOOKS AND AUDIOS BY STUART WILDE

BOOKS

THE TAOS QUINTET:

Miracles
The Force
Affirmations
The Quickening
The Trick to Money Is Having Some

❦❦❦

Infinite Self: 33 Steps to Reclaiming Your Inner Power
"Life Was Never Meant to Be a Struggle"
The Secrets of Life
Weight Loss for the Mind
Whispering Winds of Change
Silent Power

AUDIOS

Miracles
The Force
Intuition
Happiness Is Your Destiny
Loving Relationships
The Art of Meditation
Silent Power

AVAILABLE AT YOUR LOCAL BOOKSTORE,
OR CALL HAY HOUSE, INC.: AT **(800) 654-5126**

Please visit the Hay House Website at:
www.hayhouse.com

Please visit Stuart's Website at:
www.powersource.com/wilde

Silent Power

STUART WILDE

HAY HOUSE, INC.
CARLSBAD, CA

Published and distributed in the United States by:
Hay House, Inc., P.O. Box 5100, Carlsbad, CA
92018-5100 (800) 654-5126

Edited by: Leigh Robshaw and Anna Scott
Designed by: Christy Allison

ISBN 1-56170-323-0

00 99 98 97   6 5 4 3
First Printing, March 1996
Third Printing, June 1997

Printed in the United States of America

❧ CONTENTS ❧

Chapter One

THE GETTING
OF WISDOM

Every so often you meet a person who is very different. You can't put your finger on what it is that attracts you to this individual, but he or she exudes a mystery and strength, radiating a silent power that is strange and beguiling.

What is this unseen force? Why do some have it and most do not? Here in this tiny book, I'll tell you about the power, its mystery, and how to get it. There's a simple trick you have to learn. Once you've got that, silent power becomes your unspoken credential. It's a charisma that gradually grows and develops around you. Through it you can express a special goodness that helps people—and this planet—to change for the better.

From your silent power comes flow; from that flow comes simplicity of heart; from simplicity of heart comes contentment.

Some people, such as martial arts masters, gain silent power over the years anyway. They do it via emotional control and physical discipline, which quiets their energy naturally. They exude an effortless strength. Physical exercise and discipline are valuable in developing silent power, because they help you control the destructive side of the ego. But you need more than just a good physique and fitness—you need awareness as well.

Now, a little hocus-pocus. It doesn't matter if you don't believe in hocus-pocus; the basis of this concept is real enough. You don't have to worry too much about technical details. Put the intellect aside, and cut to a technology that works. That's my way.

Around you is a subtle electromagnetic body of energy that is sometimes called the subtle body and is normally unseen by the naked eye. The ancient Greeks called it the etheric body. This is where the *real* you resides. It's also where your real feelings reside.

Imagine it to be a faint energy field, like a colorless mist. But, unlike a slow, wafting mist, the etheric is moving very, very quickly. Flashing through it are mini-lightning bolts of energy, and fingers of flamelike etheric sunbursts that shoot out from you in all directions. Underlying the flashes are great waves of rolling energy that move up and down and sometimes outwards, tumbling and turning in response to emotion. You walk inside an amazing glowing bubble of light that sometimes projects three to four feet away from you in every direction.

The etheric is fascinating and beautiful to watch. I find it very humbling—the *secret* human is all there to see, spiritually naked in his or her identity. In that vulnerability dwells the very essence of our human experience—painted in the electromagnetic flashes, wisps, and lightning bolts that are projected from you.

In the etheric, you see how the human condition is complicated by the ego/personality, but you can have a deep compassion for it. For a human is not just a mind, a body, or an emotion—it is light. The brilliance of that human light overshadows the personality traits and weaknesses that come from human frailty.

In the vitality of the light is the sacrosanct identity of the eternal spiritual being. The presence of this wonderful gift of the etheric body grants you a silent power as ancient as time. It is the spiritual heritage that flows from your connection to the God-Force.

With a little training, you can sit and watch the fascinating etheric dance to which we all belong. I surmise that many of the great unexplained metaphysical mysteries are contained within it. Later in this book, there are several exercises to increase your etheric perception. But seeing the etheric is not as important as knowing it's there, projecting it correctly, and learning to perceive it via your subtle feelings.

After 12 years of experimenting, of watching people, I can guarantee that the light is definitely there. In fact, I have never seen an animal or a human who didn't have an etheric. On an energy level, it's the blueprint of the real human. Coming to see what works etherically and what doesn't has been a slow process for me, but it has been worth the effort, for the mysterious world of the etheric is one of the last unconquered frontiers. It's where everything is explained: hands-on healing, subliminal energy, charisma, power, telepathy, extrasensory perception, and perhaps even the mystery of life and death itself.

I am now convinced that, on a subtle level, everyone is subliminally aware of the etheric. When you reach out with your mind and touch other people's energy, they feel it. Often they turn around, blink, or respond in some way. They react, even though they don't know why. When two people meet, you can watch an etheric process take place. A synapse fires across the empty space between the individuals; the energy of each mingles momentarily with the other, exchanging trillions of pieces of information in a split second.

We have each had the experience of others reacting to us; often there seems to be no logic to it. But, in fact, people do pick up on our subtle energy, and even if they can't see it or put it into words, they feel it and, subliminally, they know. They vote yes, no, or maybe, according

to the qualities and strength of the energy we project.

The power of your etheric is made up
of several factors: the speed at which it
oscillates, the intensity of the energy
(how much is happening at any one
moment), and the consolidated or contained nature of the field. In an untrained
person, his or her etheric is flashing its
wispy fingers of energy out all over the
place—touching others, interfering with
them, often sucking energy from others,
impinging on them. The speed is slow-
ish, the intensity is weak; sometimes it is
torn, usually through an excess of drugs
and alcohol, and has no solid definition.
It reacts a lot to emotion, wobbling and
slopping about like an enormous pile of
jelly on a plate—rocking, rolling in jerking spastic motions, back and forth.

Of course, you don't have to see the

etheric in order to work on it, repair it if it's damaged, and make it strong. Because it expresses what you are, it's affected by your whole state of being, including your physical condition, your mental and emotional balance, and your fortitude. All this is manifest as a sense of well-being—how alive you feel, how secure you feel, and how you view the eternal spiritual self that dwells within.

So the first step to the mystery of silent power is to strengthen your psychological and emotional attitudes. This will boost your sense of well-being. It will also help you externally, as people will see from your body language, by what you say, and by your general attitude, that you are strong. Intellectually, they will *think* you're strong, but inwardly—at the subconscious level—they will feel and *know* that you are strong. They will automatically react positively. People like controlled strength; it makes them feel safe and supported.

Come—let's start by considering what power really is, and then we'll discuss leaning and not leaning. I'll show you something obvious, something that 99 percent of the population don't see.

Chapter Two

THE POWER HUNGRY—
THE POWER STARVED

What is normally considered to be power is not real power at all. Chasing money, glamour, sex; wanting control over others—political and military power—are all manifestations of the ego. They are often glorified forms of showing off; they dwell in the currency of the ego, and they often appeal only to other egos, so they are subject to people's whims. A person can be rich and successful and still be very weak. Money doesn't give you real strength; it just keeps you comfortable while you experience your dysfunction. The world of the ego is brittle, fragile, and insecure; it never feels really safe, and it has no lasting worth. The ego's world dies. More often than not, it self-destructs.

With the explosion of the mass media and the information superhighway, glamour, hype, and showing off have replaced true worth. The 32-second sound bite is more important than real facts. A glossy, skimmed-down version of life is all anyone has time for, as each vies with the other for a momentary place in the sun.

Many people are victimized by their

egos; they feel power-starved, and so they crave to be special. Of course, everyone is special in their own spiritual way, but the mass media has heightened people's need to seek fame and attention. Thirsting for power, in the ego's sense of power, they go through the ludicrous chase of trying to be important, trying to become special in the eyes of others, seeking praise, seeking status. This frenetic chase destroys and saps their energy.

Because the ego is insecure, its fears need to be quelled, so it dominates our psychology, firing off endless demands. It desperately wants things—right now—that will help it feel better. We are programmed as children to make the ego important and to try to keep it happy, and this mesmerizes us into reacting to its every need.

We don't realize that controlling the

ego through discipline is a lot simpler than trying to satisfy it all the time. By gratifying the ego, one may get a fleeting respite from its craving and demands, but then it's on — on to the next gratification. The ego always wants more.

It's life on the mouse wheel, each trotting as fast as possible to stay in the same place. Endless effort, misspent on illusion. You can see why people are programmed into it — they are psychologically immature. It's all a bit sad.

"Trying to Be Someone" comes from an insecurity, which stems from the ego's need for observers and admirers. It needs acknowledgment and stimulation to feel solid. But leaning psychologically and emotionally out into the world — demanding to be noticed, trying to be cool, seeking approval and acceptance, trying to impress, seeking praise and respect—creates imbalance and weakness. It is, in fact, an affirmation that says, "I'm not okay. I need others to approve of me in order to feel secure." By leaning psychologically, you weaken yourself. Imagine constantly leaning forward at a severe angle, reaching out—you are perpetually poised, heading for a fall.

Trying to win people over and hoping the world will accept you for your wonderfulness is futile and weak. It destroys your real power; the stress of it can make you ill. Even if you get what you want, it rarely lasts. Today's success becomes tomorrow's rejection. Leaning psychologically is a fault; it undermines what you are. Gradually you become the manifestation of other people's reality—subject, of course, to all their fickle whims, moods, and power trips. By accommodating the ego in this way, you drift from the real spiritual you that dwells with-in—which is contained and solid—to a *fake* you that is brittle, self-indulgent, and powerless.

You can tell people how marvelous you are, and a hundred others can sing your praises and pump your worth, but all that is PR and hype. In the end, you are only worth the etheric feeling you exude. That is a spiritual, metaphysical reality; everything else is illusion and dysfunction. If you want to be accepted, accept yourself. If you want to be acknowledged, acknowledge yourself. Simple.

Let's leave hype and clatter, which are weak, and head to the less obvious—silence—where consolidation and real strength lie.

Chapter Three

THE SILENT
CONSOLIDATION
OF POWER

et's talk about psychological consolidation, then on to other practi-
cal ideas for solidity and calm.

My martial arts teacher says that
when people go through the motion of
walking, what they are doing, in effect, is
going through a controlled fall. They

lean forward with their upper bodies and throw out a leg just in time. That's why even a small crack in the pavement can tip them over.

Psychologically and emotionally, life is the same as walking for most people. They constantly lean into life, yearning, dreaming, pining. They are often dissatisfied with what they are and with what they have. Instead, they seek someone or something to lift them up. They want to be declared *special*—they want life easy, delivered on a plate.

In the process of leaning, they trash their emotional balance and drift from one gratification to another. They exist at the edge of their balance and their ability to control. One adverse condition—a casual remark, a small setback—and their energy collapses. Psychologically and emotionally, they fall on their noses.

The initial point in consolidating your silent power is to discipline yourself to stop leaning. When you are the most desperate to lean in on people, that's when you should exercise control. The game is called: "Stand Straight in Life." Not many have heard of it.

First, don't lean toward things you don't have. Affirm, visualize, and take action instead.

Second, try not to lean into the future by talking or thinking about it constantly. Instead, take time each day to make the "now" special, honoring what you do have and what you have achieved. Avoid what I call plan-itis. Endlessly making plans and talking about them—"one day, someday..." trashes your power and gets you nowhere—no results and no action.

Third, start to design your life so that you don't require things from others. Try to need only those things you can get yourself. And don't suck on people emotionally or intellectually.

When you lean psychologically or emotionally on people or toward them, it's a sure sign of insecurity. It makes others feel uncomfortable. They resent the weight you are laying on them, and they will react by denying you. They don't like your self-indulgence, and your insecurity reminds them of their own vulnerability; it rattles them. Animosity builds.

Consciously and subliminally, they sense the weakness your leaning creates. It robs them of energy and crowds them; they have to buy into your needs and emotions when they would prefer to concentrate on their own. They don't like the imposition, and often they react negatively, even if they don't say so.

Alternatively, they accept the imposition of your weight, but then they feel they can take advantage of you emotionally, sexually, or financially. They will feel empowered to use you or deprecate you or discredit you in some way. Remember, when your energy touches others, they subliminally know if you are weak or strong—it affects how they see you.

I'm sure you know what I mean. Visualize someone who leans on you. Replay in your mind the emotions and the thoughts that their leaning generates in you. Remember how you react to their sometimes desperate needs. Notice how often they rob you of your energy, how in minutes you feel exhausted.

Don't do that to others; it disempowers you. A little unemotional leaning in some circumstances can be okay—others may feel pleasure in supporting you or assisting you. But too much leaning, and they will vote "no."

It does not mean that you can't ask for help—sometimes you can—but there is a difference between asking dispassionately for help and constantly leaning on others emotionally, demanding that they ameliorate your inadequacy or insecurity.

Thus, an important first step in silent power is *don't lean*. It's obvious, but most don't know it. When you are frantic for people, your needs have an air of desperation—they weaken you and push things away from you.

Have you ever had a romantic relationship where the other person was all over you like a hot rash, desperate for you? What did you do? Probably, for the first few days you enjoyed the attention, but on day three you gave this man or woman a hard time and you started to tow him or her around by the nose. You enjoyed that for a bit, but in the end, this desperation and insecurity bugged you; eventually you tossed this person out. When you're in love and you crave someone, if this individual keeps his or her distance or retreats from you, then your desire increases. If this person advances too far forward, your desire lessens, or may dissipate completely. When you are desperate for a deal and you lean into it, you push it away and/or you wind up paying more. It's called "wanting-it" tax. Before every deal, take a moment in the hallway to remind yourself that you don't need it. If you don't get it, it doesn't bother you. If you do get it, it will be under your terms, and you won't pay too much.

Even if your natural tendency is to

lean into people—because, let's say, you are a very social person—*don't* lean. Make that a discipline. You can be social without leaning in. Put a sign on your refrigerator door: "When in doubt, lean out!"

Silent power often requires the contrary approach. When others lean, step back; when they cry out, remain silent; when they run, you walk. Stay in control and exude stability, even if you don't feel too sure of yourself just yet. Don't show your weakness. Be strong. Be brave. Internalize any disquietude, and work on it later. Initially, you may not be completely solid inwardly, but you can still come across as solid externally. The inward power comes as you act out and affirm your strength and control.

Through your solidity, you help others feel secure. They seek you out, life gets easier, and it feels much better. Become the sage, remain composed, be silent, stand straight etherically. Stay inside what you know—be content, don't have too many needs. Work on yourself.

Anyway, you are probably stronger than you think. Many of the people you meet may initially seem solid. But they soon expose themselves, and you can see that they are, in fact, in silent crisis—victims of their egos. Their real power is weak and polluted. It leaves them open and exposed to the ups and downs of life. They will constantly seek to etherically borrow energy, sucking on any life force they can find. They will have house plants that die and pets that get sick a lot.

There is a law in physics that allows subatomic particles to borrow energy for just a millisecond. The particle moves temporarily to a faster orbit, but an instant later it has to repay the borrowed energy; it falls (decays) to its ground state—a slower oscillation that it can more comfortably sustain.

Etherically, humans follow the same laws. You can borrow energy from another, but you can't inherit it perpetually. A small boost, and then back you go to where you were before.

Etheric suckers grab your power as you pass them. It depreciates you. At a deep, subconscious level, they drag you away from life and closer to death. However, before you get too indignant, I have to tell you that we all pull energy from others occasionally, especially when we are tired or emotionally drained. As your energy sinks, it's human to reach for the nearest life raft. In answer to your question, "How do I protect my energy?," I've included a few ideas in Chapter Nine. Meanwhile, let's return to silent power for the moment.

People don't resonate silent power because, for most, the overriding issue in life is security. The ego's function is to keep you focused on staying alive—everyone is out and about trying to do just that. The issues of security dominate your psychology, everything you do, and much of what you say. It undermines your strength.

Everyone is silently preoccupied and worried about something, so the etheric energy is diffused and disconcerted, in some more so than in others. People worry about death and violence; they worry about *things* changing or dying, not just their bodies. Anything that has the potential to change worries them— the death of a relationship, the death of a job, the death of a daily rhythm that they are used to, the death of a privileged position, and so on. As I said in my book, *Weight Loss for the Mind,* it's the death of things that scares people.

The mind functions in this way: "If this relationship falls apart, I'll fall apart, my job might go, and with it my lifestyle, and following that, my body may change from alive to not alive." At a deep subconscious level, an argument with the boyfriend becomes a threat—a life-and-death struggle—not just a discussion about the dispute in question. That's why people can get so upset about things that seem trivial. There is an energy war going on, each seeking to preserve their etheric life force while, consciously or subconsciously, they are in a titanic struggle with the demons of insecurity.

When they are not worrying about

dropping dead, they are usually thinking about themselves, preening the ego with self-satisfying thoughts, brushing its little tail and generally making themselves as special as possible. If they aren't thinking about themselves, they are talking about themselves, keeping others amused with thrilling concepts of life in the slow lane. More often than not, they are calling on you to listen, to notice and acknowledge them, to observe them. It can be exhausting. Don't you do it to others.

Stay inside your power where you feel the most secure. And work on controlling the ego. Discipline it, so that you move from its fragile world to the immortal certainty of spirit. There you will feel the eternity within you, and your insecurity will gradually melt. You'll accept life as you find it, rather than struggling against it, and you'll know that there's no death and no failure. So accept the comings and goings of life, and flow to your highest good with little resistance and great joy.

The more you control your emotions and the reactions of your personality, the more consolidated and powerful your etheric becomes. Once your etheric energy is no longer jerking back and forth, wobbling and squirming and falling over itself, a gracious solidity develops around you. Now you'll be able to see through your own etheric, to the world of pure energy beyond. A quantum leap takes place within, and a great perception descends upon you. But, remember, silent power is a strength you quietly express, not one you wield. It's born from the seeds of self-control.

The *Tao Te Ching* says:

> *To understand others is to have*
>   *knowledge;*
> *To understand oneself is to be*
>   *illuminated.*
> *To conquer others needs strength;*
> *To conquer oneself is harder still.*
> *To be content with what one has is*
>   *to be rich...*[1]

[1] From *The Way and Its Power,* by Arthur Waley. George Allen & Unwin Ltd., London, 1934.

Chapter Four

SILENT TALKING

Part of learning not to lean is to get control of your dialogue. Most people talk too much, and what they do say is often just noise or irrelevant gibberish designed to keep themselves entertained. One of the keys to silent power is to control your need to talk. The rules of this consolidation are as follows:

Make it a discipline not to discuss your personal details with others. Develop mystery, silence, and a secrecy about your life. Don't allow people to know your deep, innermost self. Sure, you may have a friend you want to discuss things with from time to time. But, generally speaking, don't talk about yourself. If you have to, do so only in general terms and only when people ask you. Of course, sometimes the situation may require you to talk about yourself—for example, in an office situation where you have to describe your abilities. But, for the most part, keep quiet.

If you have to give instructions—or if you need to share your feelings when setting a personal boundary with another person, perhaps—choose your words carefully. A powerful person doesn't waste words, doesn't waffle and drift, but instead, thinks through what he or she wants to say and expresses these thoughts succinctly and purposely. The most powerful way to speak is with brevity.

Next, when engaging in dialogue with others, try to remain *underneath* them psychologically, rather than talking across them or even down to them from above. Let me explain. Talking above people is trying to make them feel inferior, pushing yourself onto them, or attempting to force your ideas upon them. It's dominating the conversation with endless tales of your experiences—hogging the stage.

If these people say they've been to China, and you respond by saying you've been there 19 times, you are trying to get above them, and you're being combative. Sages don't need to combat.

They are eternal and infinite and a part of everything. In the "everything," there is no high or low, so they have no need to compete. They can just be. It's enough.

The Tao says, "Those who know do not speak; those who speak do not know." It goes on to say that once one has achieved self-control, "the mysterious leveling," a perception of the Infinite Self follows—whereupon life is not limited by your talking or by your need to define it, and you, in turn, are free of its definitions. Eternal.

The *Tao* talks of this process of self-control:

> "...This is called the mysterious
>   leveling.
> He who has achieved it cannot
>   either be drawn into friendship

> *or repelled,*
> *Cannot be benefited, cannot be*
> *harmed,*
> *Cannot be raised up or humbled,*
> *And for that reason is the highest of*
> *all creatures under heaven."* [2]

This means that the sage is the highest because he or she makes him/herself the lowest—by controlling the ego (the mysterious leveling)—and disappearing into the Infinite Self instead.

Most people who talk out of ego, talk to hear themselves. They are not usually interested in what you have to say. While you talk, they are waiting to respond with something bigger and better. So, you mention you're taking a vacation, and they mention every vacation they've ever been on. Those people are dreary,

[2] See Note 1.

because they are insecure, and they have to win you over by trying to impress you.

Most of what people say doesn't impress you, does it? Mostly, it bores you. If the story of their vacation is particularly interesting or amusing, or there's something to learn from it, okay. But generally speaking, when they're telling you about their vacation, they're only pleasing themselves by trying to combat with you. You're going on a vacation, but they've been on bigger, better, more expensive ones. So, be careful with your dialogue, and try not to compete with other people. If they talk about their trip to France, and you lived in France for 20 years, don't mention it. Just listen to them. That way, you start to develop a style of dialogue that is underneath people. When your ego isn't leaning, pushing, shoving, and pressing upon them, you learn more about people, and you can love them and support them. By doing so, you exhibit solidity, and strength of character. It also allows others to feel supported by your presence, which grants you a silent charisma—silent power.

Silent talking involves first watching and listening. Next, it involves projecting love to the person you're listening to, or projecting understanding or compassion. You're getting people to voice their insecurities. You're standing tall for people by momentarily subjugating your ego's needs for theirs. Sounds weird, doesn't it? Standing tall and getting underneath others. But it's really a matter of controlling your dialogue so the other person can talk and feel more secure. You don't have to dominate, because you don't have to compete. And you don't have to feel more secure—you are perpetually secure.

So, don't talk gibberish. Most people invent things, exaggerate, or they don't know what they're talking about. They rarely have a command of what's being discussed, so they'll parrot something they've read in the paper, or they'll take something they saw on TV and regurgitate it for your benefit. Most have no access to real information, so a lot of their attitudes, and the information they do have, is secondhand. Stay inside what you know. If you're an expert on something, fine. You can talk about it if people ask. But generally speaking, don't talk gibberish, and don't bother trying to impress people.

It's very difficult to impress people with words, isn't it? Even though you may have done some incredible things, the very fact that you're telling others will make them react negatively. They will compare themselves to you and either see themselves in a bad light—which may make them angry—or consider themselves better than you—so you haven't impressed them anyway. By talking to impress people, you set up a competition. It's irritating. It has certainly irritated you in the past when you've had to sit for half an hour listening to the story of someone's vacation in France.

You can imply power and knowledge by not saying much. At most, offer something such as: "Ah, yes. Certainly. I know. Uh-huh. I understand." You can exude silent strength with just a tilt of the head, by rubbing your chin, with a wry smile, or by looking people in the eye. Never forget, you are a genius until you open your mouth.

So, while others are talking, you'll watch and perceive. Notice if their eyes dilate, watch their hand movements, see if the color of their skin changes. You'll notice if they swallow or blink, watch the slight changes in the muscles of the face, notice how people shift position sometimes when they're uncomfortable. If you see their eyes shift quickly down on a diagonal, usually to the left, you'll know that's a moment of discomfort for them, that it may mean they're lying.

When you stand inside your silence, you are in touch with the feeling of the moment, you perceive and understand what is actually being said. Anyway, you can lead a conversation without saying very much, by asking simple questions. So, if you want a conversation to go a certain way, you pull it along by asking the questions that take it in the required direction. By asking questions, you're exhibiting an interest in other people, and you're supporting them. Then, if they come up with something particularly negative or express their insecurity, you can affirm positivity, you can affirm love, you can affirm life with just a few words. They might remark how terrible a situation is, and you can say, "It's not so bad. I'm sure it will resolve itself. Everything comes to pass given time." You allow them to feel that you're there for them.

Be shrewd. Resist having to present yourself on the ego's stage. Quiet yourself and watch others. As you silently observe, touch them with your feelings. Ask yourself—silently, of course—how do these people feel? What are they actually saying? What do they really want? Who are they? What is their strongest path? If asked, what is my best response?

If they ask you a question—whether you think they should go to France or take a mountaineering trek around the Rockies, for example, don't respond immediately with what you *think* might be best for them. Pause for a moment. Touch them with your feelings. Feel the response in *your* subtle feelings that is communicated to you from deep within their reality.

Everyone knows the answer to their own question, although sometimes they're not aware of it, for it lies hidden. At best, you can only tell them what they already know. Your "logical" answer will not necessarily be the correct one. By tapping into their feelings, you'll be amazed how often you come up with an answer that is neither France nor the mountains, but something completely different. Something such as, "What I feel might be best for you is to stay at home for a month, completely clean out your house, order your life, settle your bills, and get control of your affairs."

So, as you remain silent, what you're expressing is not only a humility, but a care and love for others. It's a finesse that comes from not having to lead. It's an expertise that comes from understanding that you're a spirit, not an ego.

Another part of silent talking I should mention is that once you're settled, you will learn to talk passively and equitably. Many people, feeling their disquiet and irritation with life, like to hurt others emotionally; or they are vindictive, or judgmental and critical. They shout their abuses and try to deprecate people with verbal violence. It shows them up for what they are, immature and chronically diseased. Don't use verbal violence to hurt people or to make them less. And don't be cynical.

The Cynics were an ancient Greek sect despised because of their arrogance and sarcastic contempt for sincerity and merit. They were nicknamed the dog-men (*cynic* comes from a Greek word for *dog*). The Cynics were known for their anger and their hatred of society, which they displayed by urinating publicly in the street—hence, the term *dog-men*. Don't be a dog-man that urinates on people's hopes and dreams. Remember, anybody you criticize or judge personally has to be at the very same energy level as you. If they were not at the same level, you would either not be aware of them or, being in a higher oscillation, you wouldn't bother to comment. Always try to build people up, or at least be neutral.

To deprecate others is not honorable, it's not necessary, it demonstrates your hidden anger, and it lowers your energy. By now, you should be past it.

Now, on to the more esoteric concept of silent talking. We all have the ability to silently communicate with each other. I don't just mean body language and facial signals; I mean communicating deep within. When people are talking to you, you can enter into a silent dialogue with their minds. Often what their subconscious minds tell you is not what their words are saying. There are several ways of conducting a silent dialogue. I'll give you a simple way, and one of the more sophisticated ways.

Of course, we are not used to the idea that we can access the mind of another, but once you know you can do it, it's easy. It's nothing more than just asking what you want to know. Look at the person's forehead, and extend your concentration inwards toward his or her brain, to where the memory bank is. Your mind has to be blank. Then ask your question mentally, in simple terms. It's nothing more than a mental tap of the head—the answer comes back in your mind clear as day. It will always be expressed in the present tense—their subconscious self, the real self, has no concept of the future. If the question you pose is of an intellectual nature, the answer that comes back is short and grammatical. If the question you pose would elicit a response that is more of a feeling, or spatial in its nature, the answer will come back in baby talk.

Why? Because feelings and spatial information reside in the side of the brain opposite that of the intellect. As you know, in most people it's the right brain.

The right brain has little dialogue because that is mostly the domain and expertise of the left brain. So right-brain responses are short, childlike, and usually ungrammatical: "I happy. I scare. I no like."

Try it—you will be amazed at how simple silent dialogue is. But don't use your ability to infringe on people. Just collect information, and move toward them or away from them based on their answers. Don't push them in one direction or another. At the very most, lead without leading by asking questions that allow them to find their own way.

The more sophisticated method of silent talking is this: Imagine yourself etherically stepping out of your body, and then turn to face yourself. Now your etheric body is facing the same direction as the person in front of you, the individual you're having a conversation with. Next, step back with your etheric and melt inside that person's body, keeping your concentration on his or her head, wherein the memory lies. Now, standing inside this person etherically and keeping your mind completely blank, ask him or her your silent question and exit with the answer.

Silent talking—there is more to it than I can mention in the scope of this little book, but if you ponder on it and practice, you will discover your own methods. Remember, we are all in a silent communication all of the time.

In concluding this particular discussion, let me ask you a question: When a thought goes off in your mind, whose thought is it? Most would respond, "Mine." But how do you know that a particular thought is generated by you?

How can you say categorically that it didn't come from somewhere else?

Of course, people don't ask that kind of question. We are convinced that the thoughts we generate are ours because that is the way the intellect is programmed. It doesn't care for the idea of its domain being influenced by others. Furthermore, your intellect has no experience of other people's thoughts going off in your head. So it presumes that this does not happen. Not so.

My theoretically independent thoughts and your independent thoughts only *seem* separate from each other. It's an illusion of the intellect that comes from its limited perspective and its need to feel different and separate. In fact, there is no simple way of knowing which thoughts are genuinely yours and which are not. Other people's thoughts constantly permeate your reality, jumping into your mind unannounced, masquerading as yours. You know they do.

How often does this happen: You're at a meeting, but your mind is somewhere else—maybe you're thinking about going skiing. Then the person next to you, for no obvious reason, asks if you've ever been to Aspen, Colorado. These are simple mental jumps that we've all experienced. But deep within the subconscious, you're picking up all manner of thought forms that drift in your direction. You're an antenna, and others are picking up *your* mental activity. The air is thick with a continuous flow of silent talking, flashing back and forth.

At a very deep level of consciousness, in the heart of the global mind, we are all connected. The global mind is just one molecule of consciousness, and it is in touch with every part of itself. I accepted this premise intellectually at first, but eventually I understood it, deep in my inner feelings. That is why I don't travel and teach so much anymore. I woke to the fact that I could do just as much from within the Great Quietness—and more effectively to boot. You can do the same.

Of course, people of an intellectual bent, experts in matters of mind, will tell you that silent talking is pure drivel. But they are quite wrong. They don't know because they have not seen. Once you see, you'll know. The intellect is too disconnected from the etheric life force— the eternity in all things—and it's too focused on itself to comprehend the existence of dimension and phenomena outside its frame of reference.

I must say, when people tell me that

these other worlds are phony and nonexistent, I always make a point of agreeing with them. It's a discipline of silent power not to argue. Arguing and debating is a disease of the ego—much like seriousness is a disease of the ego that comes from either arrogance or insecurity, usually both. I'm happy to leave the intellect alone. Attempting to win people over, proselytizing, trying to convince them through dialogue, is a thankless task. It's best to communicate inwardly and wait. Eventually they'll agree, or perhaps they won't. It doesn't matter. We have all of eternity to sort things out. The fact is, we are all inside the one collective human dream. That dream can be a nightmare or a celestial vision of exquisite beauty. 'Yuh pays yer money, and yuh makes yer choice.'

Chapter Five

THE WISDOM OF *NON-ACTION*

In the writings of the old Taoist teachers, there is a concept called *Wu Wei*, which is the notion of *non-action*. Initially, it's hard to understand. Wu Wei teaches that through non-action, the sage gains everything—that in quietude, meditation, and emotional serenity, the sage gains a knowledge of the God-Force, of the eternal Tao. And in that eternity, he or she has everything, so there is no need to struggle or push to gain respect and material things.

In the modern environment, Taoist simplicity doesn't work so well. We usually have to maintain ourselves and pay the rent; we have to participate in modern experiences that were not available in 500 B.C. when the Tao was written. We have incarnated at this particular time to experience the wonders of the modern world. We need those experiences in order to grow. So non-action, in the modern context, needs to be slightly modified. We can take the *spirit* of the Taoist Wu Wei, however, and put that into our life as a further consolidation.

Wu Wei is effortless flow. The concept becomes obvious when we compare the difference between striving and working. Striving is leaning emotionally into a goal, a target—yearning for it, feeling pressured by your lack of it—tearing around like a chicken with its head cut off, trying to get it. That's striving.

Working is moving relentlessly toward your target, one step at a time, in an organized and disciplined way.

We can see Wu Wei, also, in the difference between effort and struggle. In my book, *Life Was Never Meant to Be a Struggle*, I discuss the fact that many people consider struggle to be honorable. It's a bit silly, really. There is nothing at all honorable about struggling. Usually, if you're struggling, there's something wrong.

There is a big difference between struggle and effort. Struggle is action laced with negative emotion—struggling to finish the job, struggling to qualify, struggling to be accepted, struggling to win people over, struggling to make ends meet.

Effort is a natural part of human existence. You can't walk to the store without effort—you will burn calories getting there, buying your groceries, and coming home. Effort is natural.

Struggle, however, is effort laced with emotion. It is not the minimal action and flow of Wu Wei.

If you find yourself struggling, immediately look to see what the underlying emotion is. Generally, you'll find that you're struggling because the goal you're trying to achieve isn't coming fast enough. For example, you might have a certain financial commitment that requires money to show up quickly. Or you might be struggling because your actions are incorrect. Sometimes you're trying to win people over or to convince them of something, and they don't want to be won over or convinced.

Sometimes struggle comes from having too many things to do—meaning that your life isn't organized. Or struggle can come from the frustration of having placed a goal into a particular time frame, only to find that life denies you.

As you learn to consolidate your silent power, you will learn to embrace Wu Wei. It is really patience and flow— moving away from resistance and toward simplicity, relentlessly moving toward your goal with awareness, adjusting your actions as need be—moving without emotion and without exerting yourself too much.

Stay within your balance and capabilities, and trust the Universal Law (the

Tao) to bring to you those things you
need. Non-action is the ability to dele-
gate, to be patient, to wait for things to
unfold naturally. It's the ability to perceive where your strongest path lies.
That isn't so difficult to do. Review your
options in a meditation, and decide
which way feels the strongest. Act on
your feelings, not only on your intellect.

Wu Wei is manifest in the ability to
turn back. Retreat can sometimes be the
most powerful tool in your bag of tricks.
It's the ability to walk away when things
aren't right, the ability to leave a relationship if it doesn't work, the ability to say
"no" when people are trying to suck you
into actions that are degrading or when
things don't fit into your ideas of spirituality, of proper action, of goodness.

When you can say "no," you are free.
When you *have* to have the job or you

are obliged by need to act in a certain way, when you have to win somebody's friendship, when you have to have five thousand dollars by next Tuesday, you're not free. You're in prison.

So, Wu Wei is accepting life and not forcing it. It is being aware of the ebb and flow of the seasons, aware of the spirituality of all things, aware that in the great abundance of the God-Force, there is no time. It is knowing when to act, and not acting until you know. You can wait forever if you have to. You are eternal.

Wu Wei is being content with what you are, with who you are, and with what you have *now*. It's knowing that abundance, and experiences and relationships of real worth, come only when and if you're settled. When you're balanced, the universe provides; more will always be there. But Wu Wei is the act of not pushing, not forcing.

Be the silent, controlled person who is moving relentlessly towards freedom and away from restriction—toward your goals, one step at a time, in an organized, patient way.

Wu-Wei is also the ability to get around the blocks you experience as you try to materialize ideas and goals.

When life doesn't want to dance to your tune, start by asking yourself these questions: Am I in the right place? Am I too early or too late? Am I going too fast? Do I need more patience?

Do I need time to consolidate, to create an energy within myself that is compatible with my goal? Am I trying for something that's too far in the distance? Do I need to set a goal closer to where I am now?

Ask yourself: Is what I want appropriate? Does my plan infringe on other people? Does it require them to be something they don't want to be, to do things they don't want to do? If I'm involving other people, what's in it for them? (Maybe the resistance comes from the fact that you've forgotten to include them.) Have I looked after and honored everybody—made sure they are happy and ready to perform? Is what I want self-indulgent? Will it assist me in growing and becoming a better person, in achieving a more fulfilling life? Or am I just indulging myself?

Remember, many of the things you want are, in fact, dead weights—prisons you create for yourself. More often than not, material things weigh you down— because you have to look after them and worry about them.

Sometimes the deeper spiritual part of

you, the infinite self within, protects you
from disaster. You'll head off, trying to
achieve something that the inner spiritual you, the deeper subconscious self,
doesn't actually want. So it will make
sure you arrive too late, or the person you
seek will not be there, or the check
bounces, and things generally don't work.

If things really are not working, and
they turn out to be a mess, you have to
think, Hey, is this because of something
deep inside me—do I really want what I
think I want? Am I committed to the idea
or not? What are the consequences,
obligations, and energies involved? Am I
investing too much of myself in the idea?
Perhaps it won't mean much to me when
I get it.

I'm sure you've had the experience of
going for something and getting it, then
realizing that the prize wasn't worth the

energy you expended; it was a disappointment. So be careful that you don't hurtle off up some path just to prove what a hotshot you are, without thinking through your actions, whether they actually do anything for you.

The other question to ask yourself is: Are my actions powerful and appropriate? A few small, powerful actions are worth a hundred hours of diddling about.

There's a school of thought that says: When faced with an obstacle, whack your head against it until the thing breaks. Then move to the next obstacle, and whack it with whatever part of your skull still remains. I'm not keen on that idea; it seems to lack finesse.

When you're faced with an obstacle, step back and take a long, hard look at what it is telling you. More often than not, you can adapt and walk around it.

Sometimes you have to wait while you raise your energy enough to flow over the obstacle effortlessly.

Don't whack your head against it. Stop. Get inside your power. Plot how you're going to get around it, how you're going to materialize the sales you need, for example, and how you can more effectively present your information to people.

No, don't use your head to power yourself forward, by whacking it on things. Instead, use it silently, to feel out where your strongest path lies. That is silent power.

From non-action, let's go to the silent, subtle nature of feelings.

Chapter Six

DEVELOPING
SUBTLE FEELINGS

As I said in Chapter One, we each emit a subtle etheric feeling. It has a precise identity, like a thumbprint, patterned in a complex web of energy. People perceive your consolidated power subliminally, and they respond accordingly.

The subliminal feeling you exude is

the *real* you. Life responds precisely and exactly to the subliminal feeling you emit. That's why sometimes your mind expects one thing, and life gives you something else.

There is a subtle metaphysical definition of *feeling* that is slightly different from the one you might be used to. If you tap the back of your hand with your knuckles, the impulse of that touch goes to the brain—and we call that "feeling." However, the impulse of that tap is really a *sensation,* not a feeling.

When tackling a problem, the intellect might say, "I feel we should do this or that." But the mind doesn't mean: "I feel." What it means is: "I think." Most of what the mind says it feels is not really feeling at all—it's opinion.

We refer to our emotions as feelings. But that is not a precise definition either.

Our emotions are, in effect, *reactions,* which are generated by the positive or negative responses of the ego/personality. The personality establishes rules. When life complements those rules or ideas, the personality is happy (positive emotion). When the personality is contradicted by circumstances, it is unhappy (negative emotion). If your personality doesn't like you getting cold and wet, and you fall in the river, that generates an emotional response. Emotions are the reactions of the personality, presented on a grand stage and scripted in the theater of the mind. Free tickets at the front desk for all basket cases!

Emotions are the outcropping of opinions and preferences. If you had no opinions or preferences, life could not contradict you, and you could not experience negative emotion. Of course, the

key to serenity is not necessarily in satis-
fying your ego's preferences. Rather,
it's in *reducing* your preferences and
absolutes.

Real feelings, secret feelings, origi-
nate in the etheric and develop as you
control the mind. They reach through the
quiet mind to the infinite knowing that
resonates in the eternal co-existence of
all things. There, you find the telltale
imprint that each human mind leaves
behind. In there is the metaphysical
explanation for all human action.

The memory bank of this Greater
Knowing records the history of our
human emotions—individual and collective—at the deepest level of spiritual
evolution. The total record of you is in
there. People consider such intimate
knowledge about others to be forbidden
information. They find it scary, due to its

seemingly magical and extrasensory nature. In fact, it's a natural part of our greater memory—our divine memory— to which you are connected via the God-Force. You cannot be denied access to anything you wish to know, about anyone you care to observe. Providing, of course, that the information is contained in that greater memory, you can retrieve it. So, you can't discover a scientific formula that has never been invented, but you can see how people feel, at any one precise moment, even if they are at a distance. The process may seem occult and extrasensory but, in fact, it's an *inner-*sensory perception. It's available to all, and comes from metaphysical sophistication, consolidation, quietude, and control.

The global memory, to which we all belong, resonates its own precise collective feeling, so we evolve inside a *group* feeling. Everything exudes the God-Force, even inanimate objects. In addition, everything that comes into contact with human beings is imbued with the subtle imprint that our thoughts, emotions, and etheric mark upon the object.

Nothing much is lost, but sometimes it changes. If you play a CD, the music given off imprints on the walls of the room. Each sound wave is layered one upon the other. Eventually, we might be able to scrape off the sounds and replay conversations from hundreds of years ago. The mental/emotional imprint a human being makes in the greater memory of humanity is thousands of times easier to access than a sound wave on a wall. You can access anyone's imprint and know the most intimate details about him or her. By looking inside the infinite mind, you will know. But most can't see it—because they don't know the imprint is there, and because they're too obsessed with *self,* too cluttered.

Imagine a human with a 90-piece brass band playing on her head. The *"Oompah, Oompah"* is so loud that she can't concentrate on anything else; she's living in the center of a mental tornado. Her ego is strong, her personality dominant—all subtle feelings are swamped. The *personality* prefers to hear, see, and feel things that please it, or endorse it. The *mind* focuses on what is congruent with its desires, and eliminates everything else. Perception is thus narrowed by selection.

If you want to access the mysterious global memory and expand your silent power, here's what you need to do:

First, close down the chatter of the mind—with meditation, discipline, and mental control. Fasting is good; the mind goes quiet when you don't eat. You might also try a "talking fast" for 24 hours, during which you don't allow yourself to talk. Silence, time on your own, physical exercise, and a light, low-protein, low-volume diet all help in the general raising of your energy. Discipline gives you confidence, serenity, and power.

Next, start to exercise your perception by commanding your mind to notice everything, even the most inconsequential of details. It's part of the discipline of going from asleep to awake. Train your mind to reclaim the subtlety of perception which, over the years, you have programmed it to disregard. Our ancient, atavistic abilities were lost when life became too cozy and the intellect so dominant. Stake your claim to the subtle power.

Try this: Go to a shopping mall, find a bench, and sit. Make a mental note of every minute detail of your surroundings. By telling the mind that you want to notice and remember things, you force it to concentrate on life outside, rather than on itself. The "sixth sense" of inner knowing comes, initially, from a heightened sensitivity and sense of awareness of the *usual* five senses.

Watch everything at the mall. So if I were to ask you an hour later, "What color is the trash bin outside the ice-cream parlor?," you'd know—and you'd remember if it was full or empty. And you'd say to me, "Stu, I also remember the little tag on the bin that says, 'Acme Trash Bins of Minnesota,' and there was a Snickers wrapper stuck on the north side of the bin, held by pink gum three inches from the top—next to the scratch mark that says, 'work sucks'."

"Good," I'd say, "and how many light fittings are there in that part of the mall?" And you'd respond, "17," because you'd counted them—and you'd remember that three bulbs were blown out.

Now, turn your attention to the passersby. Watch them carefully. Don't judge them, just observe. Before we get into how the people feel from an emotional, metaphysical stance, let's really notice how they look, and what that means.

How a person looks is often the same as how they feel. Over the years, your face changes to reflect your predominant emotions. So, scared people have scared eyes. Meanness shows up as an unusually thin upper lip and narrow eyes. Arrogance is in the upward tilt of the chin, and between the underside of the nose and the upper lip.

Anger is at the top of the nose. See if the bridge of the nose is pulled up—notice if the gap between the eyebrows is furrowed. Look, also, for restriction and pain in the lines around the side of the eyes. You'll also see anger in the shoulders. Angry people are curved around themselves as they try to protect their angry hearts—partly because they know subliminally that their negative emotions are likely to stop their hearts real soon, and partly to protect themselves from the pain they experience there.

Overt sexuality leans back in the upper body because the hips are tilted back. It can thus offer or show the pelvic area by thrusting it ever-so-slightly forward. When sexual look-at-me types walk, they must rotate over the top of each hip bone—first left, then right—to compensate for the forward-thrusting pelvis. The motion is ducklike and comical to watch. I know they mean no harm by it all, and watching the pelvic waddle of sexual seekers offers endless fun and entertainment—a real pantomime.

The other thing that will amuse you is the fact that humans don't think anyone is watching or noticing—obsessed as they are with themselves—and are therefore unaware. They don't imagine that you can see right through them. In the whirl of mental activity, the personality is blinded and imagines that nobody else can see either; it feels safe.

People make all sorts of tiny, surreptitious movements—movements that they are either unaware of, or that they believe are private to them. Their subconscious urges and needs, and the mental activity such urges create, show up in the muscles as minute body movements. It gives people away.

Your walk, your posture, and the expression and shape of your face provide an external blueprint of your inner self. People who are weak and insecure have a defensive upper-body posture, their eyes shift left and right, up and down, more rapidly and more often than a solid person. If you meet any true sages in the mall, you'll notice that their eyes move slowly, casting back and forth, or they will look straight ahead. Information situated to their immediate left and right will be picked up via their peripheral vision, which will have become powerful over the years.

To develop perception, you only have to ask yourself for information that you don't normally seek—visual and auditory information and, of course, we can learn a lot by how people smell. We don't usually think of smelling others unless a person has terrible BO. But as you exercise that sense, you become more and more sensitive to odor, and you'll notice that each person's is quite distinct. It tells you things.

As you heighten your perception by watching, you learn very quickly—and now you're ready to heighten your subtle feelings.

Come, let's look at the extrasensory part of your silent power that dwells inside your nature-self.

Chapter Seven

INSIDE THE
NATURE-SELF

The *nature-self* is a term that describes your deep inner spiritual connection with the plant, mineral, and animal kingdom. Embracing this understanding is a part of the wider concept of silent power. Your body is made of stardust. You are alive because a star was born and died many billions of years ago; it gave you life. The iron in the hemoglobin in your blood traveled trillions upon trillions of miles through space to play a vital role in sustaining your metabolism. The iron in your blood is over 15 billion years old. In fact, you are a reincarnation of that dead star at a higher level of evolution. The rocks, the earth, the animals, all the creatures of the earth plane, are made of that same stardust. But we are not just interconnected because we are made of the same material; we are also interconnected spiritually.

I believe that inanimate objects, as well as animals, insects, and plants, all have a spiritual evolution. I believe that there is a collective spirit for the water rat, a collective spirit for the ant, a collective spirit for the eagle, and so on. Each species evolves and grows just as you evolve and grow. The nature-self

describes your metaphysical intercon-
nection to all things physical.

You are a part of a great evolutionary
story. Even though you are human, you
have not completely left the lower evolutions of, say, animal; and you are not
denied access to the higher realms of
spirit, because a part of you is already
there. In fact, you are spread across what
may turn out to be countless dimensions
that are hovering across eternity—growing, suspended in the greater understanding of the perpetual, omnipresent, infinite self.

The evolution of the animal kingdom
is a pristine, humble evolution—one of
pure spirit, uncluttered by ego. The animals have much to teach us in their
ways. They remind us of a time when
natural simplicity and flow reigned,
before the modern era when the ego was

crowned king of this physical dimension.

In the concept of silent power and your growth, it is vital to expand your awareness across these lesser dimensions. Silently draw upon the spirits of nature—calling upon them to heal you, to instruct you, to show you the simplicity and sacredness of their ways. You can stand by a tree and pull the energy of the tree through you to cleanse your body etherically. You can rest by a lake, and use the lake to heal your confusion, anguish, and disquietude. You can use the power of a thunderstorm when you wish to perceive a higher destiny for yourself; or the power of fire to cleanse your ideas and emotions, and transmute them to a higher place. And of course, there is the power of earth—sitting upon the earth and pulling up its heat, its energy from deep within its core.

The core of this planet, in its motion of spinning, acts like an electric motor. It gives off a vast amount of power. It's your power once you discover it.

As part of the greater understanding of the nature-self, there is also a responsibility that few people are aware of. It's the responsibility to project energy to those spiritual evolutions, such as the animals, that are oscillating more slowly than we are—let's say, vibrating in a less complicated way. So we love and honor the spirits of nature—the various species of trees, the things that crawl in the ground, the denizens of water, and the birds—to pull them up and help them grow.

Just as the dimensions above offer you healing, serenity, and freshness, so you can offer the animals a heightened evolution. When you concentrate on an animal, or touch it, it evolves. When you concentrate on the plants, the things in the water, and in the air, they grow. Just by loving a bird and watching it as it flies, its evolution is enhanced. So, through the nature-self, we create a spiritual bridge—a way out of the mental, emotional, physical existence—a way back to the lesser evolutions and a way forward to the greater evolutions above us. You construct an infinite bridge across dimensions of the divine self, through the silent self.

When you are part of the elements, and part of the etheric, you are straddled across several evolutions—human and nonhuman. The beauty of the nature-self is aligned with the seasons, aligned with temperance and calm, with an eternal, infinite evolution. It is there, in the nature-self, that you experience the eternal Tao—the simplicity of all things. It is through nature that you pass and evolve at death, returning your stardust back to the earth once more.

So, in aligning to and honoring the nature-self, we understand the deep, spiritual evolution of water, earth, air, and fire—and, of course, the sacred etheric dimension. Bless the hierarchies of spirit and the group souls of the animals, and ask them to teach you. And in return, offer them love, and help them beyond where they are now—just as something or someone loved us humans eons ago and helped us evolve to where we are today.

Be gracious. Bless the lesser spirits and assist them. In this way, you empower your journey from ego to spirit, from clutter to clarity, from uncertainty to the consolidation of silent power. Be gracious.

Chapter Eight

EXTRASENSORY
ETHERIC
PERCEPTION

To view the etheric, you need good peripheral perception. In the center of the eye are the cells known as the cones—they are used to perceive direct light and color. The cells at the side of the eye are known as the rods—

they are color-blind but very much more sensitive than the cones. Over tens of thousands of years, we human beings have lost our peripheral perception, because we don't need it to keep us safe in the forest anymore.

The etheric is too faint and moves too fast for the cones to see. It's subtle. And because it's hard to see in bright sunlight and strong artificial light such as neon, the etheric is best seen in diffused light or the light of dusk.

You develop peripheral perception by engaging it—which is nothing more than telling yourself you want to reclaim that perception—and periodically focusing your attention on what is to your left and what is to your right. Place your hands to either side of your face, about 18 inches away; pull them back behind you, and watch them simultaneously, without moving your eyes to one side or the other. See how long it takes before they disappear. By activating your peripheral perception, you will, in time, see the etheric.

The other thing that helps is to have a more rarefied diet. It increases your sensitivity. So, if your diet is very light or vegetarian, you become more aware of the subtle energies of life. The other way to see the etheric is to fast. As you fast, your brain waves start to slow down, your metaphysical energy quickens; and as your metabolism slows, your mind goes quiet. Fasting takes you out of the ego's consciousness of survival, and you begin to straddle metaphysical dimensions.

The first of these is the etheric. Quieting your energy allows you to see out from within your own bubble of energy to the energies of others.

I have found that merely desiring to see the etheric doesn't work. To see it, you have to become an etheric being. Joining on an energy level, so to speak— existing in two worlds—moving your consciousness from ego to spirit, from finite to infinite.

In addition, I've noticed that believing in oneself and believing in these mysterious inner worlds helps a great deal in opening the etheric door for you. In the early days, I thought I believed, and then I hoped I believed, but some years later, I *knew* that I believed. That helped.

However, you don't have to learn to see the etheric in order to be aware of it, because you can *feel* it.

You can reach out and touch people. It's the act of moving your etheric or a part of it, with the force of your will. I know it to be true because when lying down in trance, you can, for example, direct your etheric legs to move downwards, and you will feel them drifting through the floor. It is not a sensation in the normal sense, as your physical legs are motionless. Your perception of the movement of your etheric legs is neither thinking nor emotional reaction—it's real feeling.

Back to the mall—sit on a bench where people go past, and get ready to touch their feelings etherically as they walk away. The reason you don't do it as they walk toward you is that you don't want to be unduly influenced by the way people look or how they are dressed.

The process is one of reaching *into* people. As a person passes you, visualize yourself with an elongated arm. Reach into the person through their center back, and grab a molecule of their feelings from the area of the heart. Keep your mind blank, have no preconceived opinion; just ask yourself: How do they feel? The first answer that jumps into your mind is the correct one.

Start by looking for evidence of simple emotions: anger, fear, confusion, boredom, happiness, and joy. Later, more complex mixtures come to you, and you'll start to discover intimate details as well as the more obvious stuff. Don't feel limited by a lack of perception. It doesn't matter if you're right or wrong. In the act of reaching out, you heighten your perception by demand. It's a numbers game. Try it on 500 people, and then on 10,000. Eventually you won't have to stretch to touch people— you'll know just by looking at them. It's an astonishing process. Through it you learn a great spiritual lesson; it makes you very humble. This human evolution evokes great awe.

Distant viewing: When people are not present, it is a little more tricky, but it comes with time. The best results come when the person you are viewing is asleep, preferably in the penultimate 90-minute cycle of a night's sleep. The second-last sleep cycle is usually at a deep level of brain-wave speed, where people are closest to their spiritual self—their truthful self—uncluttered by intellect. If a person wakes normally at, say, 6:00 in the morning, your best time would be between 3:00 and 4:30.

Remember, this person is a thumbprint of feeling, so to find him (or her) you have to remember how he *feels,* not how he looks. It helps to focus in the right geographic direction, but it is not vital. Now, direct your attention onto the target and ensure that your mind is blank. Pull him back toward you rather than traveling to him or moving your consciousness toward him. In the inner worlds, everything is reversed—left to right and right to left—and there are some strange laws about backwards and frontwards. Mentally stand him up in front of you. How does he feel? What is his overall emotion? What's the answer to the question you want to know? Wait for his inner self to mentally answer you. It is open and truthful and will always respond. Get your answer and let the person go, wishing him love and well-being and good strength.

Distant viewing is a subtle art. It comes from silent power as you grow, as you know that you evolve inside a global molecule of feeling, which is infinite.

Silent power offers you access to many worlds. I can't go through them all in the scope of this little book, but I can give you a clue and leave you at the crossroads, so to speak. First the discipline, then the crossroads.

The discipline: See the world as energy, and become responsible for *your* energy. Realize that everything you do, say, and touch, everything you pass— even for a fleeting second—is affected and changed by you. You impact the animals and plants; the air, water, and buildings; and people—the energy of each drops or rises to reflect the subtle etheric pressure you place on it.

When you are angry, you impress that upon the house plants, and they start to die. When you are fearful, the dog sucks that up via its etheric and gets sick. When you are mean and vindictive, the energy of the room you are in starts to wobble and act chaotically. It metaphysically starts to implode. Anyone standing nearby will be robbed of energy and pulled down. Everything gets sucked into the vortex of your negative implosion. External reality shrinks and disappears—for you, anyway. That's why car wrecks are common when a person is in a rage. Their perception of external reality is lost—they are momentarily blind, they can't see oncoming cars, and reality whacks 'em broadside.

With perception comes responsibility. Understand that if you are infinite you are everywhere, and you can be anywhere, and you are *inside* all things, and you affect them. Enough said.

The crossroads: Remember that the solidity of the world is an illusion created by the speed at which atoms oscillate.

If they slowed down just a little, you'd be able to walk through walls. In an out-of-body experience, you have consciousness inside a subtle body that we believe weighs four grams. You can pass right through the wall.

In effect, physical reality is both opaque and ethereal—just a collective feeling. You are a feeling. It's only by habit that you consider yourself solid. In a sense, you are a collection of particles, but once out of the emotion of the world, you are no longer observable; you are less solid. You transmute from being in the solid-particle state of physical existence to the more ethereal wave state. (See my book, *Whispering Winds of Change,* for an explanation of the metaphysics of particle-wave functions.)

In the wave state, you are an amorphous oscillation, existing at no particular place in space or time, with no particular human definition. That wave state contains your consciousness and can be driven by your force of will. So, through it you have an immense potential to exert yourself on the etheric reality of the global feeling. The wave can move, so you move. It's everywhere, so your mind can be everywhere. Silent talking takes you to all parts of the global feeling simultaneously. And it's simpler and cheaper than promos, hype, and the air travel needed to communicate with people's intellects.

Chapter Nine

PSYCHIC
PROTECTION

A few words in passing on psychic and etheric protection. It's hard to mount a solid protection from the mental, emotional, and sexual projection of others. So much of the etheric world is beyond our ken, and we are all inside the same one molecule of the global mind and its collective emotion.

We are all one-and-the-same human energy—in a metaphysical way, our destinies and our energies are intermixed.

However, when two people pass each other at close proximity, I have seen the etheric of one get pushed away by the other. So I came to these conclusions: If you are solid, well defined, and in emotional control—with a good sense of your Infinite Self—you have a confidence that brings a solidity to your energy, as distinct from the chaotic pattern that is normally projected. Your defense lies in consolidation and silent strength. And in being disciplined and well contained. Other etherics will not interfere with yours—they'll bounce off as you pass.

In addition, if you project love for humanity and have little resistance, incoming energy often passes right through you—it has no place to attach. Because of your spiritual perspective and the love you project, your oscillation is not congruent with the lower depreciating energy of the ego's world. For example, if you are celibate or you project no sexual energy, it is impossible for another to hold a sexual visualization of you for more than a fleeting moment. The thought form slides away like a knife point pressed onto a slippery surface.

Your best defense is to have little criticism and judgment of others, and no rancor, hatred, or animosity. The best defense is to have nothing to defend. The more you are not locked into reality via criticism and definition, the more opaque you become. It's a type of invisibility. You are here and not here, in the evolution and distant from it. Trust in the Great Goodness to keep you safe. It will.

Finally, it should be part of your daily discipline to silently project love and peace to all whom you meet. As you pass people on the street, look them in the eye and silently say "love," and press that love into their hearts. Do that to everyone without fail, and gradually you will develop a resounding sense of unconditional acceptance. That's the best protection.

Chapter Ten

CONCLUSION

I know it's hard to exude confidence if you don't feel completely solid. But you can fake it 'til you make it. Just by maintaining silence—not leaning, not pushing, not yearning—and controlling your emotional reactions, you dominate your psychology. You act out a silent strength even though you may not be resonating it deeply within as yet.

Don't give yourself away. Work quietly on your weaknesses, develop a reserve and mystery, be organized and self-sufficient, and keep your life to yourself. Knowledge is power. The knowledge you never speak of is silent power.

Consume less, stay in control, be at one with your inner self and nature. Purify your life, constantly skimming, cleaning, throwing things out, simplifying. One morning you wake up and the power is all there. You won't have to cover up your disquietude—it will have melted away.

A great unfolding awaits you as you begin to understand that you can dominate this human evolution of yours, even from a humble position. You don't have to be a superstar. In fact, the superstars often show their weakness by having to stand out and preen themselves and strut, to mask their worries and insecurities. Most of the *"rah-rah"* is there to cover up an inner self that's none too solid.

Do this: Draw a line in the sand. Agree to step across to a new way of dealing with life. Set up a sacred week for yourself. Pray to your God, and call on your Infinite Self and the nature spirits and all the great powers to help you make the changes your need. Meditate each day, fast for a day or two during the week, also pick 24 hours during which you'll maintain complete silence.

Read, bathe, rest, purify, walk in the forest at night, pull energy from the earth, become friends with water; let the spirits of the air blow away any confusion. Use the strength of fire to give you a new hope and courage, and ask it to grant you a vision of the future. Let it show you how the God-Force can warm your heart and how it will empower your detachment so you can consolidate your serenity, and your poise.

And you—yes, you—you long-lost scallywag, it's time for you to come back to the sacred place to which you belong, and step inside the gentle embrace of the Great Goodness.

Remember, there was a time eons ago when our people had perception—before it was lost in clatter, insecurity, and self-delusion. Claim that perception as yours, and learn to touch the etheric, use the life force, and rekindle the old ways within you so that others might remember, also. Step now to an alternative evolution, beyond hesitancy and fear, beyond the common emotions; step now to that pristine place within. No matter if you can't see it as yet. Believe and walk in. It will welcome you, I assure you, and it will teach you in the years to come.

There is much there for you to learn—strange aspects of this incredible journey that few really understand. Worlds inside worlds, opaque dimensions of spiritual evolution folded in on themselves, moving backwards in time. Creativity as yet unseen, hovering just beyond the intellect, waiting to be gathered up and expressed. Much wisdom and many things await, not the least of which is the great awe that pours forth from an eternal perception of self.

And, in your sacred week, pray for yourself and pray for all humanity and the animals and the little things, and ask that the Great Spirit descend upon us all. Ask it to help us restore a sacred, silent power. Ask it to open our eyes, so that over time the light flowing from the Great Goodness will establish a world of simplicity, bathed in the kindness of a settled heart—each human spirit gracious, respectful; and each contributing in his or her humble way to the greater understanding of this strange but glorious human experience.

The world of the ego will change in the coming decades and, over a few hundred years, a new perception will rise from the burnt-out ashes of this evolutionary phase. People will want to return to the sacred ways of long ago—it will seem natural and proper. Eventually we'll see a world steeped in honor and balance, dressed in the unassuming vestments of unconditional love and serenity.

Embrace your silent power. Come. Be brave. A great awakening is yours for the asking. Then, offer your perception and silent power in service to others. Be subtle; don't force people. Teach by example. Lead them from behind, gradually, with a touch here and a word there. Lead them from their pain, out of the darkness, across the invisible bridge, to the land of perpetual light wherein dwells the enormity of the Great Goodness, waiting patiently for each to arrive.

Come. Step. Your time is now.

Bestselling author and lecturer
Stuart Wilde is one of the real
characters of the self-help, human
potential movement. His style is humor-
ous, controversial, poignant, and trans-
formational. He has written 11 books,
which have been translated into 9 different languages.

INTERNATIONAL TOUR AND SEMINAR INFORMATION

For information on
STUART WILDE'S
latest tours and seminar
dates, contact:

WHITE DOVE INTERNATIONAL
P.O. Box 1000, Taos, NM 87571
(505) 758-0500 (phone)
(505) 758-2265 (fax)

Stuart's Website:
www.powersource.com/wilde

We hope you enjoyed this
Hay House book. If you would like to
receive a free catalog featuring additional Hay House books and products,
or if you would like information about
the Hay Foundation, please contact:

HAY HOUSE, INC.
P.O. Box 5100
Carlsbad, CA 92018-5100
(800) 654-5126
(800) 650-5115 (fax)

Please visit the Hay House Website at:
www.hayhouse.com